THE GREAT BIBLE DISCOVERY

JEREMIAH - THE COST OF BEING A PROPHET

THE BIBLE IS A BEST-SELLER. IT IS ALSO ONE OF THE MASTER-WORKS OF WORLD LITERATURE - SO IMPORTANT THAT UNIVERSITIES TODAY TEACH 'NON-RELIGIOUS' BIBLE COURSES TO HELP STUDENTS WHO CHOOSE TO STUDY WESTERN LITERATURE.

THE BIBLE POSSESSES AN AMAZING POWER TO FASCINATE YOUNG AND OLD ALIKE.

ONE REASON FOR THIS UNIVERSAL APPEAL IS THAT IT DEALS WITH BASIC HUMAN LONGINGS, EMOTIONS, RELATIONSHIPS. 'ALL THE WORLD IS HERE.' ANOTHER REASON IS THAT SO MUCH OF THE BIBLE CONSISTS OF STORIES. THEY ARE FULL OF MEANING BUT EASY TO REMEMBER.

HERE ARE THOSE STORIES, PRESENTED SIMPLY AND WITH A MINIMUM OF EXPLANATION. WE HAVE LEFT THE TEXT TO SPEAK FOR ITSELF. GIFTED ARTISTS USE THE ACTION-STRIP TECHNIQUE TO BRING THE BIBLE'S DEEP MESSAGE TO READERS OF ALL AGES. THEIR DRAWINGS ARE BASED ON INFORMATION FROM ARCHAEOLOGICAL DISCOVERIES COVERING FIFTEEN CENTURIES.

AN ANCIENT BOOK - PRESENTED FOR THE PEOPLE OF THE SECOND MILLENNIUM. A RELIGIOUS BOOK - PRESENTED FREE FROM THE INTERPRETATION OF ANY PARTICULAR CHURCH. A UNIVERSAL BOOK - PRESENTED IN A FORM THAT ALL MAY ENJOY.

M publishing
CARLISLE, UK

13

In art galleries and cathedrals, it is easy to identify the figure of Jeremiah. He is 'the weeping prophet'. This tradition is based on one of his sayings but in any case Jeremiah had good reason to weep.

He saw the people of Judah ignoring God's love and laws. He realized the nation was heading for disaster. When he warned the people they not only ignored him but even tried to kill him. Among his enemies were the inhabitants of his own village. He might have gained strength from a wife and family but this happiness was not for him. At times he even wondered whether the God he served was deliberately deceiving him.

This 'weeping prophet' also showed amazing strength and courage. Although tempted to give up his ministry as a prophet, he did not do so. He spoke out for God in spite of all the opposition he faced. Right at the end of his life we see him choosing to share the fate of his fellow-Judaeans, refugees in Egypt. Perhaps the one ray of hope to shine on Jeremiah may have come when the Book of Deuteronomy was discovered and King Josiah reformed Judah's religious practices. Sadly, Josiah died young and his successors were wicked or weak - sometimes both. In any case, the reforms seem to have affected only the outward worship of the nation - not the hearts of its people.

Jeremiah learned not to place any trust in religious rituals or buildings - not even the Temple and its worship. Yet he looked forward to better times. In particular, he spoke of a day when God would make a new covenant with his people. At Sinai God's law had been written on stone. Under the new covenant, said Jeremiah, it would be written on their hearts. And God would forgive their sins (Jeremiah 31:31).

We know that Jesus valued Jeremiah's prophecy. On the night when he was betrayed he quoted from Jeremiah, using words which today are heard all over the world. He spoke of a cup of wine as representing 'my blood of the new covenant, shed for the forgiveness of sins'.

JEREMIAH
2 KINGS 21-25
2 CHRONICLES 33-36

JEREMIAH - THE COST OF BEING A PROPHET

13

First published as Découvrir la Bible 1983

First edition © Larousse S.A. 1984
24-volume series adaptation by Mike Jacklin © Knowledge Unlimited 1994
This edition © OM Publishing 1995

01 00 99 98 97 96 95   7 6 5 4 3 2 1

OM Publishing is an imprint of Send the Light Ltd.,
P.O. Box 300, Carlisle, Cumbria CA3 0QS, U.K.

Introductions: Peter Cousins

British Library Cataloguing in Publication Data
A catalogue record for this book is available from the British Library
ISBN 1-85078-217-2

Printed in Singapore by Tien Wah Press (Pte) Ltd.

JEREMIA
KING JOSIAH'S REFORM

Carchemish • Haran • NINEVEH • ASSHUR
Riblah • Damascus • Tigris BABYLON → Euphrates
Megiddo • JERUSALEM
MEMPHIS

SCENARIO : Etienne DAHLER
DRAWING : Victor de la FUENTE

AT THE BEGINNING OF THE 7TH CENTURY BC, AFTER KING HEZEKIAH OF JUDAH AND THE PROPHET ISAIAH HAD DIED, THE KINGDOM OF JUDAH, LIKE ALL THE NEAR EAST, WAS CONTROLLED BY THE ASSYRIANS.

THE ASSYRIAN KINGS, FIRST ESARHADDON, THEN ASHURBANIPAL, EVEN CONTROLLED EGYPT.

THIS TIME THE WHOLE OF THE EAST IS OURS!

IN 663 ASHURBANIPAL SACKED THE CITY OF THEBES, THE FAMOUS CAPITAL OF THE PHARAOHS.

3

MANASSEH, SON OF HEZEKIAH, BECAME KING IN JERUSALEM WHEN HE WAS 12 YEARS OLD. HE WOULD HAVE THE LONGEST REIGN IN THE HISTORY OF JUDAH.

WE MUST GIVE IN TO THE ASSYRIANS... AND WE MUST ALSO ACCEPT THEIR GODS.

BUT, MANASSEH...WHAT ABOUT OUR GOD, THE LORD?

HE WILL JUST HAVE TO SHARE HIS TEMPLE WITH THE OTHERS!

...AND WOODEN STATUES OF IDOLS WERE SET UP IN THE TEMPLE IN JERUSALEM.

WHAT A TERRIBLE THING! IF KING HEZEKIAH COULD SEE THIS...

NOT SO LOUDLY! YOU COULD PAY FOR SAYING THAT!

DO YOU KNOW WHAT HAPPENED TO THE WORKMEN WHO REFUSED TO DO THIS?

...ASSYRIAN SOLDIERS KILLED THEM IN THEIR WORKSHOP.

KING MANASSEH WENT IN FOR MAGIC AND FORTUNE-TELLING.

MAGICIAN, WHAT DO YOU SAY ABOUT THIS?

THOSE WHO ARE FAITHFUL TO THE LORD HATE YOU! THEY'RE PLOTTING AGAINST YOU...

I THOUGHT AS MUCH... BUT MOLOCH WILL PROTECT ME.

AND, NEAR TO JERUSALEM, KING MANASSEH...

MOLOCH, I'M SACRIFICING MY OWN SON TO YOU! PROTECT ME FROM ALL HARM!

SO THE GOD OF ISRAEL SENT PROPHETS.

BECAUSE OF THE TERRIBLE THINGS THE KING HAS DONE, I WILL BRING GREAT TROUBLE TO JERUSALEM...

...I WILL ABANDON THE REST OF MY PEOPLE; I WILL LEAVE THEM IN THE HANDS OF THEIR ENEMIES!

KILL ALL THESE PROPHETS!

KING MANASSEH WAS FURIOUS. HE GAVE AN ORDER.

AND A TERRIBLE SILENCE FELL OVER JERUSALEM.

BUT NOTHING STOPPED THOSE WHO WERE FAITHFUL TO THE LIVING GOD.

SO WE CAN'T PREACH THE WORD ANY LONGER? VERY WELL, THEN! LET'S WRITE IT DOWN!

WAS THIS PERHAPS HOW THE GREAT TRADITIONS, WHICH BEGAN WITH MOSES AND ARE FOUND IN THE BOOK OF DEUTERONOMY, WERE WRITTEN DOWN?

...SO, TOO, THE WORDS OF THE PROPHETS AMOS, HOSEA, ISAIAH, AND MICAH.

DAUGHTER OF ZION,* SUFFER AND GROAN LIKE A WOMAN IN LABOUR. YOU WILL LEAVE THE CITY, TO LIVE IN THE FIELDS, AND YOU WILL GO AWAY AS FAR AS BABYLON. (Micah 4:10)

* Jerusalem.

6

IN 642 BC KING MANASSEH DIED. HIS SON AMON BECAME KING. HE HAD A YOUNG SON, *JOSIAH*, 6 YEARS OLD.

BUT TWO YEARS LATER THE NEWS SPREAD THROUGH THE TOWNS AROUND *JERUSALEM*.

THE KING HAS BEEN ASSASSINATED! KING AMON IS DEAD!

...WHICH MADE THE PEASANTS VERY ANGRY.

WE CAN'T ALLOW THE LINE OF DAVID TO DIE OUT!

HE'S RIGHT! LET'S GO TO JERUSALEM!

KING AMON'S MURDERERS HAD TO GIVE IN TO THIS PEASANT REBELLION...

...AND LITTLE JOSIAH, AMON'S SON, WAS PROCLAIMED KING.

HE'S VERY YOUNG! ONLY 8 YEARS OLD!

IT'S UP TO US TO TEACH HIM ABOUT THE TEMPLE.

THE PRIESTS OF THE TEMPLE IN JERUSALEM TAUGHT THE YOUNG KING JOSIAH, SO THAT HE GREW UP IN THE WAYS OF GOD...

THIS MORNING I'M GOING TO TELL YOU HOW GOD GAVE THE LAW TO MOSES.

A FEW KILOMETRES FROM JERUSALEM, IN THE VILLAGE OF ANATHOTH, ANOTHER YOUNG LAD WAS BEING BROUGHT UP IN THE OLD WAYS.

JEREMIAH, MY SON, NEVER FORGET THAT WE ARE THE DESCENDANTS OF ABIATHAR, THE HIGH PRIEST, DAVID'S FRIEND...

...BUT HE WAS BANISHED TO THIS VILLAGE BY SOLOMON... THAT MEANS WE CAN'T EVER SERVE IN THE TEMPLE AGAIN.

FATHER, MAY I GO AND HELP THE WORKERS?

YES, IF YOU WANT TO.

BUT, JEREMIAH, AREN'T YOU A PRIEST?

SO? MOSES WAS A MOST HUMBLE MAN, DAVID WAS A SHEPHERD, AND AMOS A FARMER.

THE PRIESTS OF JERUSALEM DON'T LOVE US, BUT ALREADY YOU'RE THE KIND OF MAN GOD WANTS.

JEREMIAH LIVED IN ANATHOTH FOR 20 YEARS - 20 YEARS OF PEACE.

THEN ONE DAY...

FATHER, I MUST SPEAK TO YOU.

THAT SOUNDS VERY SERIOUS!

YOU SEE, I'VE RECEIVED THIS WORD FROM THE LORD: BEFORE I FORMED YOU IN YOUR MOTHER'S WOMB, I KNEW YOU; BEFORE YOU WERE BORN, I CHOSE YOU TO BE A PROPHET TO THE NATIONS.

AND HOW DID YOU ANSWER?

I SAID: LORD GOD, I DON'T KNOW HOW TO SPEAK! I'M MUCH TOO YOUNG!

GO TO THE PEOPLE TO WHOM I SEND YOU. TELL THEM EVERYTHING I COMMAND YOU.

BUT THE LORD SAID TO ME:

THEN THE YOUNG PROPHET WENT TO JERUSALEM.

JEREMIAH WALKED THROUGH THE STREETS OF THE CITY.

THEY'VE REJECTED ME, THE SOURCE OF LIVING WATER, AND DUG OUT RESERVOIRS...
SAYS THE LORD...

...CRACKED RESERVOIRS THAT DON'T HOLD WATER!

THE LORD SAID TO ME: WALK AROUND JERUSALEM, AND FIND ME ONE PERSON WHO DOES WHAT IS RIGHT AND TRIES TO BE FAITHFUL...

JUST ONE! AND I WILL FORGIVE THE CITY!

BUT THEY'VE ALL TURNED AWAY FROM THE LORD... SO JERUSALEM WILL BE DESTROYED LIKE SODOM AND GOMORRAH IN THE TIME OF ABRAHAM.

JERUSALEM! HEAR THE VOICE OF GOD, SO THAT HE DOESN'T LEAVE YOU, AND YOU BECOME A DESERT!

BUT JEREMIAH WASN'T THE ONLY ONE TO BRING BAD NEWS. **ZEPHANIAH,** A YOUNG PRINCE OF THE HOUSE OF JUDAH, PREACHED THE WORD OF THE LORD...

WOE TO JERUSALEM, CITY OF INJUSTICE! SHE DOESN'T LISTEN TO ANY WARNING! SHE REFUSES TO TRUST GOD!

ZEPHANIAH! I COULD HAVE YOU THROWN INTO PRISON...

KING JOSIAH, I HAVE SOMETHING IMPORTANT TO SAY TO YOU...

BE CAREFUL, JOSIAH! REMEMBER HOW SAMARIA FELL!

THIS IS TERRIBLE! BUT HOW CAN THINGS BE CHANGED?

ON THE DAY OF THE LORD THE TOWN OF GAZA WILL BE FLATTENED; ASHKELON WILL BECOME DESERTED; ASHDOD WILL BE DESTROYED; EKRON WILL BE LEFT IN RUINS!

AND JERUSALEM, ZEPHANIAH?

THE LORD WILL STRETCH OUT HIS HAND AGAINST HER, **AND SHE'LL BE DESTROYED.**

YES, THE GREAT DAY OF THE LORD IS NEAR – *A DAY OF DARKNESS, A DAY OF FEAR AND HORROR!*

ON THAT DAY PEOPLE WILL BE IN DEEP TROUBLE. THEY WILL GROPE ABOUT LIKE BLIND MEN, AND WILL BE LOST!

THEN THERE IS NO HOPE?

YES! THE LORD SAYS, WHEN I HAVE BROKEN THE PROUD...

...MY PEOPLE WILL BE HUMBLE AND POOR, AND THEY WILL FIND SAFETY IN ME.

THE ASSYRIAN EMPIRE WAS BECOMING WEAKER. ITS GRIP ON JUDAH LOOSENED. KING JOSIAH SPOKE TO HIS COUNCILLORS AND TO **SHAPHAN**, HIS SECRETARY...

THE PROPHET IS RIGHT. WE MUST USE THIS TIME TO REPAIR THE TEMPLE. TELL THE WORKMEN TO MAKE A START.

SOME TIME LATER...

SHAPHAN, GO AND ASK THE HIGH PRIEST TO GIVE THE MONEY THE PEOPLE BROUGHT TO THOSE WHO ARE IN CHARGE OF THE WORK.

HERE I HAVE A PRICELESS TREASURE! THEY FOUND THIS SCROLL WHILE THEY WERE WORKING IN THE TEMPLE.*

WHAT'S IT ABOUT?

* THE BOOK OF DEUTERONOMY, FOUND BY ACCIDENT.

IT'S THE LAW OF THE LORD!

INCREDIBLE!

SHAPHAN HURRIED BACK TO KING JOSIAH'S PALACE...

LISTEN, ISRAEL: THE LORD IS OUR GOD! THE LORD IS THE ONLY GOD!

GO ON!

YOU WILL BREAK DOWN ALL THE HIGH PLACES... YOU WILL DESTROY THE ALTARS... YOU WILL BURN THE IDOLS...

THE VOICE OF GOD!

IF YOU DON'T LISTEN TO THE LORD, TERRIBLE THINGS WILL HAPPEN TO YOU!

SHAPHAN, STOP!

GO AND ASK THE LORD ABOUT THIS BOOK... HE MUST BE VERY ANGRY WITH OUR FATHERS AND WITH US.

THEN SHAPHAN AND THE HIGH PRIEST WENT TO SEE THE PROPHETESS HULDAH...

STAND BACK! LET US PASS!

THIS IS WHAT THE LORD SAYS: I WILL BRING TROUBLE ON THIS PLACE AND ON THE PEOPLE WHO LIVE HERE. I WILL DO EVERYTHING THAT IT SAYS IN THE BOOK YOU'VE BEEN READING TO THE KING.

BUT SAY TO THE KING: BECAUSE YOU LET MY WORD TOUCH YOUR HEART, YOU WON'T SEE THESE TERRIBLE THINGS. YOU'LL DIE IN PEACE.

KING JOSIAH WENT TO THE TEMPLE IN JERUSALEM, AND ORDERED THE PAGAN PARTS OF THE WORSHIP TO BE TAKEN AWAY.

THE ASSYRIAN GODS WERE QUICKLY TAKEN OUT OF THE TEMPLE...

...AND THROUGHOUT THE KINGDOM THE PLACES OF IDOL-WORSHIP WERE DESTROYED.

SEEING THAT ASSYRIA WAS BECOMING WEAK, JOSIAH TOOK THE CHANCE TO RECAPTURE THE TOWNS IN THE NORTH OF THE KINGDOM.

AND JOSIAH CONTINUED TO DESTROY THE ALTARS TO IDOLS, KILLING THOSE WHO SACRIFICED THERE.

FOR A TIME JEREMIAH DID NOT PROPHESY. HE WENT TO VISIT THE PROPHETESS HULDAH.

JEREMIAH, WHAT DO YOU THINK ABOUT ALL THAT'S HAPPENING?

I'M AFRAID THAT JOSIAH'S REFORMS ARE TOO LATE. **THE LORD WANTS THE PEOPLE TRULY TO TURN BACK TO HIM.**

BUT THAT YEAR THE PASSOVER WAS CELEBRATED AS IT HAD NOT BEEN FOR A LONG TIME.

LET'S REMEMBER ALL THAT THE LORD HAS DONE FOR US, AND HOW HE SET US FREE FROM SLAVERY!

BUT THE MIDDLE EAST WOULD SOON BE CAUGHT UP IN A GREAT CONFLICT: THE BABYLONIANS AND THE MEDES WERE LINING UP AGAINST ASSYRIA, WHICH FORMED AN ALLIANCE WITH EGYPT.

NINEVEH

ASSHUR

Megiddo

JERUSALEM

BABYLON

I AM MAKING THE BABYLONIANS POWERFUL... THEY'LL INVADE THE LANDS OF OTHER PEOPLES!

IN THE KINGDOM OF JUDAH NEW VOICES WERE HEARD...

ONE DAY THE LORD SAID TO ME: **HABAKKUK**, WRITE DOWN THIS VISION ON CLAY TABLETS...

BUT WHILE THE BATTLE RAGED, THE PROPHET HABAKKUK TURNED TO ASSYRIA, AND SHOUTED...

...BECAUSE YOU'VE PLUNDERED MANY NATIONS, ALL THE OTHER PEOPLES WILL PLUNDER YOU!

AS YOUR SPEEDING ARROWS FLASHED AND YOUR SHINING SPEARS GLEAMED, THE SUN AND THE MOON STOOD STILL.

LORD, YOU MARCH ACROSS THE EARTH IN ANGER, IN FURY YOU TRAMPLE THE NATIONS. YOU GO FORWARD TO SAVE YOUR PEOPLE.

IN 614 BC THE MEDES AND THE BABYLONIANS CAPTURED ASSHUR, THE OLDEST CITY OF THE ASSYRIAN EMPIRE.

THE EXILES FROM THE NORTHERN KINGDOM, WHO HAD BEEN PRISONERS OF ASSYRIA SINCE THE FALL OF SAMARIA, AT LAST BEGAN TO HOPE AGAIN. JEREMIAH HAD SPOKEN ABOUT IT.

ISRAEL, DON'T BE AFRAID! I'M GOING TO SET YOU FREE FROM THE DISTANT LAND. JACOB WILL COME BACK, AND ENJOY REST AND PEACE.

RETURN, FAITHLESS ISRAEL! I WON'T LOOK ON YOU WITH A STERN FACE ANY LONGER, BECAUSE I'M MERCIFUL.

IN 612 IT WAS THE TURN OF NINEVEH, THE ASSYRIAN CAPITAL, TO BE BESIEGED.

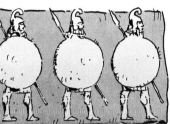

THE PROPHET **NAHUM**, A YOUNG DISCIPLE OF JEREMIAH, ANNOUNCED THE FALL OF THE CITY.

NINEVEH, YOUR DESTROYER IS MARCHING AGAINST YOU! MAN THE DEFENCES! GUARD THE ROAD! PREPARE FOR BATTLE!

THERE THEY ARE! THEY FLING THEMSELVES ONTO THE CITY, RACING THROUGH THE SQUARES, FLASHING LIKE TORCHES!

QUICKLY! THIS WAY, YOUR MAJESTY!

HURRY UP!

THAT'S IT! THE GATES ARE FORCED OPEN. NINEVEH IS LIKE A BROKEN DAM, WITH THE WATER FLOWING OUT ON ALL SIDES.

STOP! STOP!

PLUNDER THE GOLD! PLUNDER THE SILVER OF THE ASSYRIANS!

NINEVEH IS LIKE A DEFEATED LION... NINEVEH, YOU'RE CURSED! THIS IS THE WORD OF THE LORD.

YOUR LEADERS ARE LIKE A SWARM OF LOCUSTS, WHICH SETTLE IN THE HEDGES ON A COLD DAY. BUT WHEN THE SUN COMES OUT, THEY FLY AWAY, AND NO ONE KNOWS WHERE THEY HAVE GONE.

Nahum 3:17

IN 610 AN EGYPTIAN ARMY MARCHED TOWARDS ARAM, TO HELP THE ASSYRIANS.

THE BABYLONIANS WERE THE VICTORS IN THE SIEGE OF HARAN. THE ASSYRIAN EMPIRE WAS DYING.

THE SURVIVORS OF THE ASSYRIAN ARMY FLED TO THE TOWN OF CARCHEMISH...

THE PROPHET NAHUM HAD A VISION OF THAT BATTLE.

KING OF ASSYRIA, THERE'S NO CURE FOR YOUR WOUNDS. ALL WHO HEAR OF YOUR DESTRUCTION CLAP THEIR HANDS FOR JOY — WERE THERE ANY WHO DIDN'T SUFFER FROM YOUR CRUELTY?

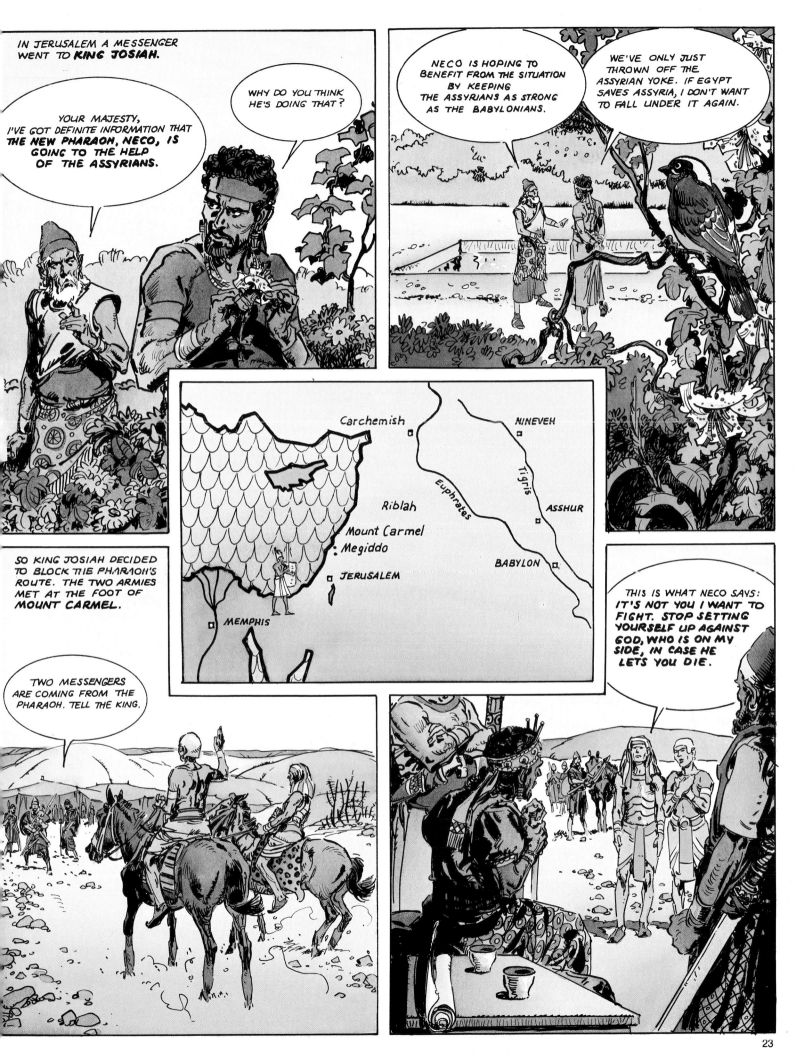

IN JERUSALEM A MESSENGER WENT TO **KING JOSIAH**.

YOUR MAJESTY, I'VE GOT DEFINITE INFORMATION THAT **THE NEW PHARAOH, NECO, IS GOING TO THE HELP OF THE ASSYRIANS**.

WHY DO YOU THINK HE'S DOING THAT?

NECO IS HOPING TO BENEFIT FROM THE SITUATION BY KEEPING THE ASSYRIANS AS STRONG AS THE BABYLONIANS.

WE'VE ONLY JUST THROWN OFF THE ASSYRIAN YOKE. IF EGYPT SAVES ASSYRIA, I DON'T WANT TO FALL UNDER IT AGAIN.

Carchemish

NINEVEH

Tigris

Euphrates

ASSHUR

Riblah

Mount Carmel

Megiddo

BABYLON

JERUSALEM

MEMPHIS

SO KING JOSIAH DECIDED TO BLOCK THE PHARAOH'S ROUTE. THE TWO ARMIES MET AT THE FOOT OF **MOUNT CARMEL**.

TWO MESSENGERS ARE COMING FROM THE PHARAOH. TELL THE KING.

THIS IS WHAT NECO SAYS: IT'S NOT YOU I WANT TO FIGHT. STOP SETTING YOURSELF UP AGAINST GOD, WHO IS ON MY SIDE, IN CASE HE LETS YOU DIE.

BUT JOSIAH WAS STUBBORN. HE FOUGHT THE EGYPTIANS ON THE PLAIN OF MEGIDDO...

...WITHOUT REALIZING THAT NECO'S WORDS HAD COME FROM GOD.

THE KING OF JUDAH WAS WOUNDED BY AN EGYPTIAN ARROW. THEY TOOK HIM BACK TO JERUSALEM WHERE HE DIED. JEREMIAH WATCHED THE SAD PROCESSION PASS BY.

JOSIAH RULED FAIRLY AND WITH JUSTICE. HE STOOD UP FOR THE POOR AND FOR PEOPLE IN NEED. DOESN'T THAT MEAN THAT HE KNEW GOD?

WE MUST ANOINT **SHALLUM**, THE SECOND SON. HE'LL KNOW HOW TO CARRY ON HIS FATHER'S POLICIES.

SHALLUM BECAME KING OF JUDAH, AND TOOK THE NAME OF JOAHAZ.

THE PHARAOH NECO HAD SAVED THE LAST ASSYRIAN OUTPOST FROM DESTRUCTION. HE SOON REMEMBERED THE LITTLE KING OF JUDAH.

KING JOAHAZ, WE'RE ORDERED TO TAKE YOU TO THE PHARAOH.

I HAVE NO CHOICE. I'LL FOLLOW YOU.

WEEP FOR THE ONE WHO IS GOING AWAY. HE'LL NEVER COME BACK.

SADLY JEREMIAH WATCHED THE YOUNG KING JOAHAZ.

DON'T YOU HAVE A BROTHER CALLED ELIAKIM?

THAT'S RIGHT!

AT RIBLAH IN ARAM THE PHARAOH NECO STRIPPED JOAHAZ OF THE KINGSHIP AND PUT HIM IN CHAINS.

VERY WELL! I CHOOSE HIM TO BE KING.

JOAHAZ WAS TAKEN TO EGYPT, WHERE HE DIED...

AS NECO HAD DECIDED, ELIAKIM BECAME KING, TAKING THE NAME OF JEHOIAKIM.

...DARK DAYS WERE COMING FOR THE KINGDOM OF JUDAH.

JEREMIA
THE FALL OF JERUSALEM

WHILE JEHOIAKIM WAS KING, THE PEOPLE BELIEVED THEY WERE SAFE SIMPLY BECAUSE THE TEMPLE WAS THERE, AND BECAUSE THEY DID CERTAIN THINGS. BUT ALL OVER THE COUNTRY THEY WERE WORSHIPPING IDOLS AGAIN.

SCENARIO: Etienne DAHLER
DRAWING: Victor de la FUENTE

JEREMIAH, THE PROPHET OF THE LIVING GOD, COULDN'T REMAIN SILENT...

THIS IS WHAT THE LORD SAYS: IF YOU DON'T OBEY THE LAW, IF YOU DON'T LISTEN TO THE PROPHETS WHOM I KEEP ON SENDING TO YOU...

...I WILL DO TO THE TEMPLE WHAT I DID TO THE PLACE OF WORSHIP AT SHILOH, AND I WILL MAKE JERUSALEM A CURSE FOR ALL THE NATIONS OF THE EARTH.

KILL HIM! HE'S BLASPHEMING!

HE SAYS HE'S SPEAKING IN THE NAME OF THE LIVING GOD, AND HE DARES TO ANNOUNCE THE DESTRUCTION OF THE TEMPLE!

IN THE TIME OF KING HEZEKIAH THE PROPHET MICAH SAID: 'JERUSALEM WILL BECOME A RUIN; MOUNT ZION WILL BECOME A FOREST.' WAS HE PUT TO DEATH FOR THAT?

THIS MAN HASN'T DONE ANYTHING TO DESERVE DEATH! BE OFF WITH YOU!

JEREMIAH, A WORD OF ADVICE! DISAPPEAR FOR A WHILE! THE KING WOULDN'T FORGIVE YOU FOR ANOTHER RIOT.

NEXT TIME WE'LL HAVE OUR REVENGE!

ALL THE SAME, JEREMIAH ISN'T GOING TO TELL US HOW TO BEHAVE.

SO JEREMIAH WENT BACK TO ANATHOTH, THE VILLAGE WHERE HE'D BEEN BORN.

THE PEOPLE THERE DIDN'T MAKE HIM WELCOME.

GO BACK WHERE YOU COME FROM, YOU BIRD OF ILL OMEN!

DON'T LOOK AT THAT MAN! HE BRINGS BAD LUCK!

SO, WOULD YOU HAVE US KILL EVERYBODY?

BUT FATHER, YOU WERE SO HAPPY WHEN I TOLD YOU THAT GOD WANTED TO MAKE ME A PROPHET...

I DIDN'T THINK YOU'D BE SAYING SUCH THINGS! ...YOU MUST KEEP QUIET NOW!

YOU'RE MAKING EVERYBODY SUFFER... ESPECIALLY YOURSELF. SETTLE DOWN TO A NORMAL LIFE NOW, WITH A WIFE AND CHILDREN...

...EVEN JEREMIAH'S MOTHER..

PERHAPS YOU'RE RIGHT...

...AFTER ALL, THE PATRIARCHS WERE MARRIED... MOSES AND ISAIAH TOO... THEY HAD CHILDREN, AND THEY SERVED GOD BETTER THAN I DO.

DON'T TAKE A WIFE OR HAVE CHILDREN, BECAUSE THEY'LL ALL DIE WITHOUT BEING BURIED, VICTIMS OF WAR OR FAMINE.

JEREMIAH KEPT COMPLETELY TO HIMSELF... HE WAS IN DESPAIR, BECAUSE HE SAW THAT NO ONE WAS LISTENING TO GOD'S WORD, AND THE PEOPLE WERE GOING TO BE DRIVEN OUT OF THE COUNTRY.

THEY SAY THAT ANYONE WHO TOUCHES HIM WILL DIE WITHIN A YEAR!

IT WOULD BE BETTER TO GET RID OF HIM!

DON'T WORRY! SOME PEOPLE ARE THINKING ABOUT THAT...

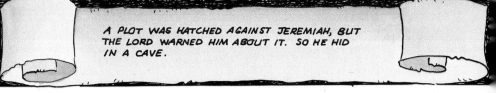

A PLOT WAS HATCHED AGAINST JEREMIAH, BUT THE LORD WARNED HIM ABOUT IT. SO HE HID IN A CAVE.

NEBUCHADNEZZAR CONQUERED MORE AND MORE COUNTRIES. WITH DANGER THREATENING THE KINGDOM OF JUDAH, **JEREMIAH RETURNED TO JERUSALEM.**

HERE, YOUNG MAN; GO AND BUY ME A POT FROM THE MAN OVER THERE.

THEN JEREMIAH SENT FOR SOME OF THE ELDERS AND PRIESTS, AND LED THEM DOWN AN ALLEY IN JERUSALEM.

WHERE'S HE GOING?

I DON'T KNOW, BUT HE'S TAKING US STRAIGHT TO THE VALLEY OF HINNOM.*

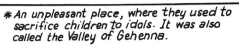

*An unpleasant place, where they used to sacrifice children to idols. It was also called the Valley of Gehenna.

THIS IS WHAT THE LIVING GOD SAYS: YOU'VE TURNED AWAY FROM ME; YOU'VE MADE THIS PLACE UNCLEAN BY KILLING YOUR CHILDREN HERE.

THAT'S WHY I'LL UPSET ALL THE PLANS OF THE PEOPLE OF JUDAH. I'LL GIVE THEIR CORPSES TO THE BIRDS AND THE WILD ANIMALS AS FOOD!

I'LL BREAK THIS PEOPLE AND DESTROY THIS CITY!

THEN JEREMIAH WENT BACK TO THE COURT OF THE TEMPLE.

THIS IS WHAT THE LORD SAYS: ALL THE TERRIBLE THINGS WHICH HAVE BEEN FORETOLD – I'LL MAKE THEM HAPPEN TO THIS CITY, BECAUSE YOU'RE STUBBORN AND WON'T LISTEN TO ME.

THERE'S JEREMIAH! THIS TIME HE'LL NOT GET AWAY!

WILL YOU BE QUIET?

SOLDIER, THROW HIM INTO PRISON!

BUT EARLY THE NEXT DAY...

YOU'RE LUCKY! YOU HAVE POWERFUL FRIENDS! COME ON, OUT OF HERE!

YOUR FAMILY WILL DIE IN FRONT OF YOUR EYES, STRUCK DOWN BY THE SWORD!

AS FOR YOU, YOU'LL BE TAKEN TO BABYLON AS A PRISONER, AND YOU'LL DIE THERE.

BARUCH BECAME JEREMIAH'S SECRETARY, AND WROTE DOWN EVERYTHING THE PROPHET SAID.

I'LL DO TO THIS LAND EVERYTHING WRITTEN IN THIS BOOK...

THE NEXT YEAR THERE WAS A GREAT PILGRIMAGE TO JERUSALEM FOR A DAY OF FASTING...

I'M NOT ALLOWED TO GO TO THE TEMPLE, BARUCH, BUT YOU GO AND READ TO THE PEOPLE WHAT I'VE DICTATED.

BARUCH DID WHAT THE PROPHET ASKED.

THIS IS WHAT THE LORD SAYS:

DISASTER WILL FALL ON ALL THE NATIONS!
A GREAT STORM IS GATHERING AT THE FAR ENDS OF THE EARTH!
MOURN AND CRY!
ROLL IN THE DUST!
BECAUSE THE TIME HAS COME FOR YOU TO BE SLAUGHTERED!

MICAIAH, THE SON OF KING JEHOIAKIM'S SECRETARY, HEARD THESE WORDS, AND RAN TO THE PALACE...

YOU CAN'T GO IN-SIDE! THE MINISTERS ARE IN A MEETING!

I MUST WARN MY FATHER! IT'S IMPORTANT...

A FEW MINUTES LATER BARUCH ARRIVED ...

'BECAUSE YOU HAVEN'T LISTENED TO ME,' THE LORD SAYS, 'I WILL SEND FOR MY SERVANT NEBUCHADNEZZAR. HE'LL FIGHT AGAINST THIS LAND, AND WILL LEAVE IT IN RUINS, A SHOCKING SIGHT!'

HOW DID YOU COME TO WRITE ALL THIS?

JEREMIAH DICTATED EVERY WORD TO ME.

YOU AND JEREMIAH, GO AND HIDE YOURSELVES, AND DON'T LET ANYONE KNOW WHERE YOU ARE!

WE MUST WARN THE KING! THERE'S STILL TIME TO AVOID THE WORST.

BUT WILL HE KNOW HOW TO TURN BACK TO GOD?

One of the king's ministers visited Jeremiah and Baruch in their hiding-place.

The next morning a strange load left Jerusalem.

Jeremiah and Baruch got down from the cart.

HUNTED LIKE ANIMALS, JEREMIAH AND BARUCH WERE SOON EXHAUSTED.

CURSE THE DAY I WAS BORN! CURSE THE MAN WHO TOOK THE NEWS TO MY FATHER!

WHY DID I LEAVE MY MOTHER'S WOMB? JUST TO SEE SUFFERING AND SADNESS, AND TO END MY DAYS IN DISGRACE?

MASTER, WE MUSTN'T STOP HERE...

I CAN'T FIND ANY REST... THE LORD IS CRUSHING ME, AND I'M NOT STRONG ENOUGH TO TAKE IT.

THE TWO MEN WOULD GO ON WANDERING FOR SEVEN LONG YEARS...

AROUND THE YEAR 602, EVEN THOUGH HE SIDED WITH EGYPT, JEHOIAKIM HAD TO GIVE IN TO THE BABYLONIAN ENVOYS.

HERE'S MY TRIBUTE FOR YOUR KING. JERUSALEM MIGHT BE ON ITS KNEES, BUT IT ISN'T BEATEN!

ORDER THE ARAMAEANS, THE MOABITES, AND THE AMMONITES TO MARCH ON JERUSALEM...

THREE YEARS LATER, COUNTING ON THE EGYPTIANS TO SUPPORT HIM, THE KING OF JUDAH REBELLED, AND REFUSED TO PAY HIS TRIBUTE. SO IN BABYLON NEBUCHADNEZZAR ISSUED HIS ORDERS.

I'LL MAKE A STOP THERE BEFORE GOING ON TO EGYPT.

JEREMIAH, BARUCH, AND THEIR DONKEY ARRIVED AT THE GATE OF A VILLAGE.

WHAT'S HAPPENING?

WE'RE ESCAPING TO JERUSALEM! THE ENEMY TROOPS ARE ON THEIR WAY...

KING JEHOIAKIM HAS JUST DIED! HIS SON JEHOIACHIN IS THE NEW KING.

THEN WE CAN GO BACK TO JERUSALEM TOO!

I'VE ALREADY TOLD YOU EVERYTHING THAT'S HAPPENING TODAY. YOU WOULDN'T LISTEN TO ANY OF IT! IT'S THE LORD'S TURN NOT TO LISTEN TO YOUR WEEPING!

JERUSALEM WAS BESIEGED.* NEBUCHADNEZZAR HIMSELF WENT THERE TO PLUCK THE CITY LIKE A RIPE FRUIT.

*In 597 BC.

KING JEHOIACHIN, I'M SURE THERE'S NO POINT IN HOLDING OUT ANY LONGER...

I AGREE. WE'LL GIVE OURSELVES UP.

OPEN THE CITY-GATES!

JEREMIAH WEPT, WHILE **NEBUCHADNEZZAR** SPARED JERUSALEM BUT TOOK THE TEMPLE TREASURE, AND SENT THOUSANDS OF PEOPLE INTO EXILE IN BABYLON.

* In Jehoiachin's place Nebuchadnezzar made his uncle, Mattaniah, king of Judah, and changed his name to Zedekiah.

IN JERUSALEM LIFE CONTINUED... POLITICS AS WELL.

YOUR MAJESTY, DON'T HESITATE! EGYPT IS POWERFUL AGAIN; WITH HER SUPPORT WE COULD HOLD UP OUR HEADS ONCE MORE.

WHAT UTTER STUPIDITY! THE BABYLONIANS ARE POWERFUL; WE MUST REMAIN THEIR SUBJECTS.

THAT WAS WHAT JEREMIAH THOUGHT TOO.

OBEY THE BABYLONIANS, AND YOU'LL STAY ALIVE! DON'T LISTEN TO THE FALSE PROPHETS* WHO TELL YOU TO REBEL! THEY AREN'T SENT BY THE LORD.

*Among them was Hananiah, a court prophet who contradicted Jeremiah's message.

THE LORD SAYS: IN TWO YEARS I'LL BREAK THE BABYLONIAN YOKE. ALL THOSE WHO WERE DEPORTED WILL COME BACK TO JERUSALEM.

HANANIAH, IF ONLY YOU WERE TELLING THE TRUTH!

HANANIAH LIFTED UP THE YOKE THAT JEREMIAH WAS WEARING.

SEE IF I'M A LIAR!

LOOK! THE YOKE IS BROKEN!

HANANIAH IS RIGHT!

IN BABYLON, TOO, SOME PROPHETS AMONG THE EXILES WERE TELLING THEM THAT THEY WOULD SOON BE FREE, BUT IN JERUSALEM JEREMIAH...

BARUCH, WRITE THIS: TO ALL WHO ARE IN BABYLON, BUILD HOUSES; GET MARRIED, AND HAVE CHILDREN, BECAUSE IT WILL BE SEVENTY YEARS BEFORE YOU COME BACK TO THIS COUNTRY!

70 YEARS?

IN SPITE OF JEREMIAH'S INFLUENCE, KING **ZEDEKIAH** WAS TEMPTED TO FORM AN ALLIANCE WITH EGYPT. IN 588 BC IT SEEMED AS IF HE HAD DONE THE RIGHT THING...

THE EGYPTIAN ARMY IS CROSSING THE FRONTIER.

THAT'S IT! GOD IS GOING TO SET US FREE!

NEBUCHADNEZZAR QUICKLY RETURNED TO JUDAH.

ZEDEKIAH, GO AND MEET HIM, AND SURRENDER! OTHERWISE THIS CITY WILL BE BURNT DOWN, AND YOU'LL DIE BY THE SWORD.

NO! WHEN JEHOIACHIN SURRENDERED, IT WAS A DISASTER FOR JERUSALEM. **THIS TIME WE'LL FIGHT!**

WITH THE EGYPTIAN TROOPS ADVANCING, NEBUCHADNEZZAR LEFT JERUSALEM TO DO BATTLE WITH THEM.

WHERE ARE THOSE WHO SAY JERUSALEM IS GOING TO BE LEFT IN RUINS?

THEY SHOULD BE ARRESTED FOR TREASON!

AND FOR BLASPHEMY!

SOMETIME LATER JEREMIAH WANTED TO LEAVE THE CITY, TO SEE ABOUT A FIELD HE HAD BOUGHT IN ANATHOTH...

YOU'RE GOING TO JOIN THE BABYLONIANS!

THAT'S A LIE! I'M GOING TO MY FAMILY.

YOU CAN TELL YOUR STORY TO THE OFFICER OF THE GUARDS!

A LITTLE LATER THE EGYPTIANS WERE PUT TO FLIGHT, AND THE BABYLONIANS RETURNED TO JERUSALEM...

JEREMIAH, DO YOU HAVE A WORD FROM GOD FOR ME?

YES, ZEDEKIAH! YOU'LL BE DELIVERED INTO THE HANDS OF THE KING OF BABYLON!

JEREMIAH, FOLLOW ME! KING ZEDEKIAH WANTS TO TALK TO YOU!

KING ZEDEKIAH DIDN'T DARE TO PUT THE PROPHET TO DEATH, SO HIS LIFE BECAME A LITTLE EASIER.

HERE, JEREMIAH! ENJOY IT! SOON THERE WON'T BE ANY BREAD IN THE WHOLE CITY!

SOON THERE WAS A FAMINE IN THE BESIEGED CITY OF JERUSALEM.
IN THE COURTYARD OF THE PRISON, JEREMIAH PROPHESIED IN FULL VIEW OF HIS GUARDS.

THOSE WHO STAY IN THE CITY WILL DIE! THOSE WHO GO OUT AND SURRENDER TO THE BABYLONIANS WILL LIVE!

OUR PRISONER IS STILL GOING HIS OWN WAY!

THAT'S ENOUGH! THROW HIM INTO THE CELL!

45

AFTER A SIEGE OF 20 MONTHS JERUSALEM FELL TO THE BABYLONIANS.*

THE LORD LIT A FIRE IN ZION THAT BURNT IT TO THE GROUND.

NO ONE ANYWHERE, NOT EVEN THE RULERS OF FOREIGN NATIONS, BELIEVED THAT ANY INVADER COULD ENTER JERUSALEM'S GATES.

(Lamentations 4:11)

*July 587.

THE NEXT NIGHT KING ZEDEKIAH FLED WITH HIS FAMILY AND SOME OF HIS SOLDIERS...

BUT THE BABYLONIANS CAPTURED THEM IN THE PLAIN NEAR JERICHO, AND TOOK THEM TO NEBUCHADNEZZAR IN RIBLAH.

NEBUCHADNEZZAR HAD ZEDEKIAH'S SONS STRANGLED; THEN HE HAD ZEDEKIAH'S EYES PUT OUT, AND TIED HIM TO THE TAIL OF HIS HORSE.

LEAVE THE PRISON, AND JOIN THE OTHERS. NO ONE WILL HARM YOU IN ANY WAY!

JEREMIAH AND THE OTHER SURVIVORS WERE TAKEN TO A CONCENTRATION CAMP AT RAMAH.

A MONTH LATER NEBUCHADNEZZAR SENT GENERAL **NEBUZARADAN** TO JERUSALEM.

PLUNDER THE TEMPLE! PULL DOWN THE WALLS, AND BURN THE CITY!

NEBUZARADAN, THE KING'S ORDERS WILL BE CARRIED OUT.

JERUSALEM WAS DESTROYED BECAUSE IT DIDN'T LISTEN TO GOD'S WORDS, SPOKEN BY JEREMIAH.

ONE DAY OUR SONS WILL COME BACK. THE CITY WILL BE REBUILT, AND SHOUTS OF JOY WILL BE HEARD.

JEREMIAH PROPHESIED AT RAMAH.

NEBUZARADAN WENT TO RAMAH TO MEET JEREMIAH.

BY ORDERS OF NEBUCHADNEZZAR, YOU'RE FREE. IF YOU WANT TO COME TO BABYLON WITH ME, YOU MAY DO SO. YOU MAY ALSO STAY IN THIS COUNTRY.

I'LL STAY!

MOST OF THE PEOPLE WERE DEPORTED TO BABYLON. THOSE LEFT BEHIND GATHERED TOGETHER...

A VOICE IS HEARD IN RAMAH. IT IS RACHEL* CRYING FOR HER CHILDREN. DRY YOUR TEARS, BECAUSE YOUR SONS WILL COME BACK FROM THE ENEMY'S LAND.

* A reference to the wife of the patriarch Jacob, the mother of Benjamin, the tribe to which Jeremiah belonged. According to tradition, Rachel's tomb was at Ramah.

...AROUND GEDALIAH, A FRIEND OF JEREMIAH, WHO WAS APPOINTED GOVERNOR.

BUT SOON AFTERWARDS GEDALIAH WAS ASSASSINATED BY PEOPLE OPPOSED TO THE BABYLONIANS.

JOHANAN, THE COMMANDER OF THE ARMY, WAS AFRAID THAT THE BABYLONIANS WOULD PUNISH THEM. SO HE TOOK CHARGE OF THE PEOPLE, AND SET OUT FOR EGYPT.

STAY IN THE LAND; DON'T BE AFRAID! IF YOU GO, NO ONE WILL SURVIVE, SAYS THE LORD GOD!

JEREMIAH, BE QUIET, AND WALK ON!

ONCE THEY REACHED EGYPT, THE PEOPLE BEGAN TO WORSHIP IDOLS AGAIN.

THE LORD SAYS: I SWEAR BY MY NAME, EVERY LAST ONE OF YOU WILL DIE HERE!

BARUCH, WILL THEY ALWAYS BE TRAITORS, RIGHT TO THE END?

TIRED OUT AND BROKEN, THE OLD PROPHET DIED...

MASTER, THERE'S STILL HOPE ... OUR BROTHERS IN BABYLON!